The Legendary

MISS LENA HORNE

STORMY WEATHER
(Ted Koehler – Harold Arlen)
(Arranged by Ned Freeman)

LENA HORNE
with Orchestra

The Legendary
MISS LENA HORNE

Carole Boston Weatherford

illustrated by Elizabeth Zunon

ATHENEUM BOOKS FOR YOUNG READERS
NEW YORK   LONDON   TORONTO   SYDNEY   NEW DELHI

ATHENEUM BOOKS FOR YOUNG READERS

An imprint of Simon & Schuster Children's Publishing Division

1230 Avenue of the Americas, New York, New York 10020

Text copyright © 2017 by Carole Boston Weatherford

Illustrations copyright © 2017 by Elizabeth Zunon

Photo of young Lena on p. 46 courtesy of the Library of Congress, Prints & Photographs Division,

Carl Van Vechten Collection, LC-USZ62-116600

Photo on p. 47: "Lena Horne conserves fuel (gas)." N.d. Randt Studios, Inc., courtesy of the National Archives

ATHENEUM BOOKS FOR YOUNG READERS is a registered trademark of Simon & Schuster, Inc.

Atheneum logo is a trademark of Simon & Schuster, Inc.

For information about special discounts for bulk purchases, please contact Simon & Schuster Special Sales

at 1-866-506-1949 or business@simonandschuster.com.

The Simon & Schuster Speakers Bureau can bring authors to your live event. For more information or to

book an event, contact the Simon & Schuster Speakers Bureau at 1-866-248-3049 or visit our website at

www.simonspeakers.com.

Book design by Ann Bobco

The text of this book was set in Neutraface 2 Text.

The illustrations were rendered in oil paint, with cut paper collage.

Manufactured in China

1116 SCP

First edition

2 4 6 8 10 9 7 5 3 1

Library of Congress Cataloging-in-Publication Data

Names: Weatherford, Carole Boston, 1956- author. | Zunon, Elizabeth, illustrator.

Title: The legendary Miss Lena Horne / Carole Boston Weatherford ; illustrated by Elizabeth Zunon.

Description: First edition. | New York : Atheneum Books for Young Readers, [2017] |

Includes bibliographical references and index.

Identifiers: LCCN 2016016139

ISBN 978-1-4814-6824-4

ISBN 978-1-4814-6825-1 (eBook)

Subjects: LCSH: Horne, Lena—Juvenile literature. | Singers—United States—Biography—Juvenile literature. |

LCGFT: Biographies.

Classification: LCC ML3930.H677 W43 2017 | DDC 782.42164092 [B]—dc23

LC record available at https://lccn.loc.gov/2016016139

To
my mother, Carolyn,
who defines beauty,
dignity, and
strength
—C. B. W.

To all
the little girls and boys
dreaming big dreams
—E. Z.

You have to be taught to be second class;
you're not born that way.
—Lena Horne

The Horne family tree was laden with achievers: teachers, activists, a Harlem Renaissance poet, the dean of a black college, and Lena's grandmother Cora Calhoun Horne, a college graduate.

Lena's father, Teddy, had other ideas.
A street hustler, he lived high on the hog,
had fine clothes and fancy cars, never went to jail,
and eventually owned a hotel and restaurant.
Lena's mother, Edna, was an actress in a touring troupe.
The day Lena arrived, Teddy bet on a card game
to pay the hospital bill.

June 30, 1917, Brooklyn. Native New Yorker
Lena Horne was born into the freedom struggle.
At two, she became not just one of the youngest members
of the National Association for the Advancement of Colored People,
but also a cover girl for the NAACP Branch Bulletin.

NAACP *Bulletin*

National Association for the Advancement of Colored People

OCTOBER, 1919

THE NAACP'S YOUNGEST MEMBERS

Lift ev'ry voice and sing,
'Til earth and heaven ring,
Ring with the harmonies of Liberty
—from "Lift Ev'ry Voice and Sing"/"Negro National Anthem"

When Lena was barely a toddler,
Teddy left for Pittsburgh and turned his smarts
to becoming a gambling kingpin.
Her stage-struck mother hit the road too.
Little Lena stayed with her grandmother Cora
in the family's four-story Brooklyn townhouse.

Cora had high standards and drilled into Lena
good manners, black pride, and the value
of a well-rounded education.
Lena learned to read before kindergarten;
books were her lifelong love,
a haven from hardship and heartache.
Cora enrolled Lena in drama and dance lessons
but would not hear of a show-business career.
Not for respectable folks, Cora said.

Cora had high hopes for her granddaughter,
but at a tender age, Lena got toted along
as her mother chased bit parts in vaudeville.
Lena lived out of a suitcase, shuttled between relatives,
boarding houses, and homes that took in children for pay.

Being on the road with her mother
was rough, especially down South.
Lena's shoes never fit
and her feet always hurt
because stores did not let blacks
try on shoes before buying.
A black cast member was lynched
and a black guest was beaten at the rooming house
where Lena and her mother were staying.
Lena longed for home.

> Sometimes I feel like a motherless child
> A long way from home
> —from an African American spiritual sung by Lena Horne

BIBLIOGRAPHY

The Associated Press. "Legendary Jazz Singer Lena Horne Dies at 92." *Billboard*. 10 May 2010. Website. (last accessed 9/21/2015) billboard.com/ articles/news/958302/legendary-jazz-singer-lena-horne-dies-at-92

Buckley, Gail Lumet. *The Hornes: An American Family*. New York: Knopf, 1986.

Gavin, James. *Stormy Weather: The Life of Lena Horne*. New York: Atria Books, 2009.

Horne, Lena, and Richard Schickel. *Lena*. New York: Doubleday, 1965.

Johnson, Reed. "An Appreciation: Lena Horne." *Los Angeles Times*. 11 May 2010. Website. (last accessed 9/21/2015) articles.latimes.com/ 2010/may/11/entertainment/la-et-0511-lena-horne-20100511

Lawrence, John. "Lena Horne: A Great Lady Who Broke the Color Line." *San Diego Free Press*. 31 March 2015. Website. (last accessed 9/21/2015) sandiegofreepress.org/2015/03/ lena-horne-a-great-lady-who-broke-the-color-line/

"Lena Horne." Masterworks Broadway. Sony Music Entertainment. 2015. Website. (last accessed 9/21/2015) masterworksbroadway.com/artist/lena-horne/

FURTHER READING, LISTENING, AND VIEWING

Haskins, James, and Kathleen Benson. *Lena: A Biography of Lena Horne*. Chelsea, MI: Scarborough House, 1991.

"Lena Horne in Her Own Words." *American Masters*. PBS. (last accessed 9/21/2015) pbs.org/wnet/americanmasters/lena-horne-about-the-performer/487/

"Lena Horne." Bio. A&E Television Network. Website. (last accessed 9/21/2015) biography.com/people/lena-horne-9344086

Palmer, Leslie. *Lena Horne*. New York: Chelsea House, 1989.

The Essential Lena Horne: The RCA Years. Sony Masterworks, 2010. CD

Lena Horne at the Waldorf Astoria. Hallmark. 2013. CD

Lena Horne: The Lady and Her Music. Warner Bros. 1995. CD

Stormy Weather. Twentieth Century Fox, 2006. DVD

Miss Horne's career was indeed in full swing when the United States entered World War II. My research into the Tuskegee Airmen, the US military's first black pilots, uncovered photographs showing how Lena Horne supported the war effort. In one photo, she is perched in the cockpit of a plane at Tuskegee's Moton Airfield. In a government photo promoting energy conservation on the homefront, she dons an apron and stands by a stove.

During the segregation era, Miss Horne took the heat of being an African American entertainer. Often she could not eat or sleep at the venues she headlined. She finally boiled over at a Beverly Hills restaurant, hurling an ashtray and a lamp at a white diner who called her a racial epithet. When she was blacklisted as a Communist by the US House of Representatives Un-American Activities Committee and was banned from movies and television, her nightclub act, fortunately, saved her career.

What was no act was Lena Horne's commitment to the civil rights movement. She not only talked the talk but walked the walk, taking a hiatus from show business to march and sing for racial equality.

In *The Wiz,* Motown's 1978 adaptation of *The Wizard of Oz,* Miss Horne made her last film appearance as Glinda the Good Witch of the South. How fitting that she played a fairy godmother of sorts! The battles that Miss Horne fought against racism and discrimination expanded opportunities for generations of black entertainers to come.

AUTHOR'S NOTE

I first glimpsed Lena Horne on television in the 1960s as my family watched the Dean Martin and Ed Sullivan shows. Back then, Horne—a regular on musical variety shows—was one of the few African Americans on the small screen. So whenever she appeared, I took notice. Later, in the 1970s, I saw her singing with *Sesame Street*'s Kermit the Frog as my younger brother watched that show.

But my real introduction to Miss Horne came from a brief biography in a book whose title I have since forgotten. With insight into her pioneering career and fighting spirit, I gained deeper respect for Miss Horne.

Around the same time, I got interested in the Jazz Age and the Harlem Renaissance. My father evoked the era for me with his record collection and his memories of live shows at Baltimore's Royal Theatre. The theater was part of the so-called "Chitlin' Circuit," which African American entertainers toured. With friends, I attended black musical film festivals in Baltimore and at New York's Lincoln Center, and viewed clips from some of Miss Horne's classic 1940s movies. Most notably, I saw her sing "Stormy Weather."

Then my father and I saw the musical revue *Lena Horne: The Lady and Her Music* at the old Morris A. Mechanic Theatre in Baltimore. Her live performance was unforgettable. Miss Horne not only sang a song; she animated the lyrics. Already an admirer, I became a bona fide fan.

By that time, I was writing jazz poetry. Miss Horne appeared with other artists in the lines of my verse. While researching pictures to accompany my poems, I came across a 1941 Carl Van Vechten photograph of a teenage Lena at the beginning of her show business career. That photo inspired me to write a poem celebrating female jazz vocalists. I still can't get enough of Miss Horne's swinging rendition of "'Deed I Do."

JENNIFER HUDSON

NATALIE COLE

Lena Horne's pioneering performances,
her fight on the front lines of the freedom struggle,
the racial barriers that she broke,
and her fiery pride form her legacy.
Because Lena refused
to darken rear doors,
black stars now gleam
on red carpets
and reap box-office gold.

THE SUPREMES

Her crown silvery gray, Lena kept cutting records
and winning praise: Grammy and Tony Awards,
a Kennedy Center Honor, honorary degrees
from Howard University and Yale,
and a place in the Big Band and Jazz Hall of Fame.

Then music saved her.
Lena remembered what bandleader Count Basie,
jazz royalty himself, had told her years earlier:
*They don't give us a chance very often,
and when they do, we have to take it.*
Lena seized every opportunity to shine.

It wasn't easy being an *EBONY* queen.
Lena's life was not without sad notes.
In 1967 she lost her dearest friend, composer
and pianist Billy Strayhorn, and in 1971
lost her father, son, and husband
all in the same year. Lena was so down
that the only way she could go was up.
She stayed in and lost herself in books.

Eventually, the star returned to the silver screen
as Glinda the Good Witch in *The Wiz*,
and to Broadway
in an award-winning one-woman show.
Lena even sang on *Sesame Street*
to a certain green frog.

She took time off from the stage and screen
to join the civil rights movement.
She sang at rallies for
the National Council of Negro Women.
At the March on Washington, where Dr. King
gave his famous "I Have a Dream" speech,
Lena spoke one word into the microphone:

Freedom!

In this battle,
Lena was not just a pretty face;
she was a foot soldier.

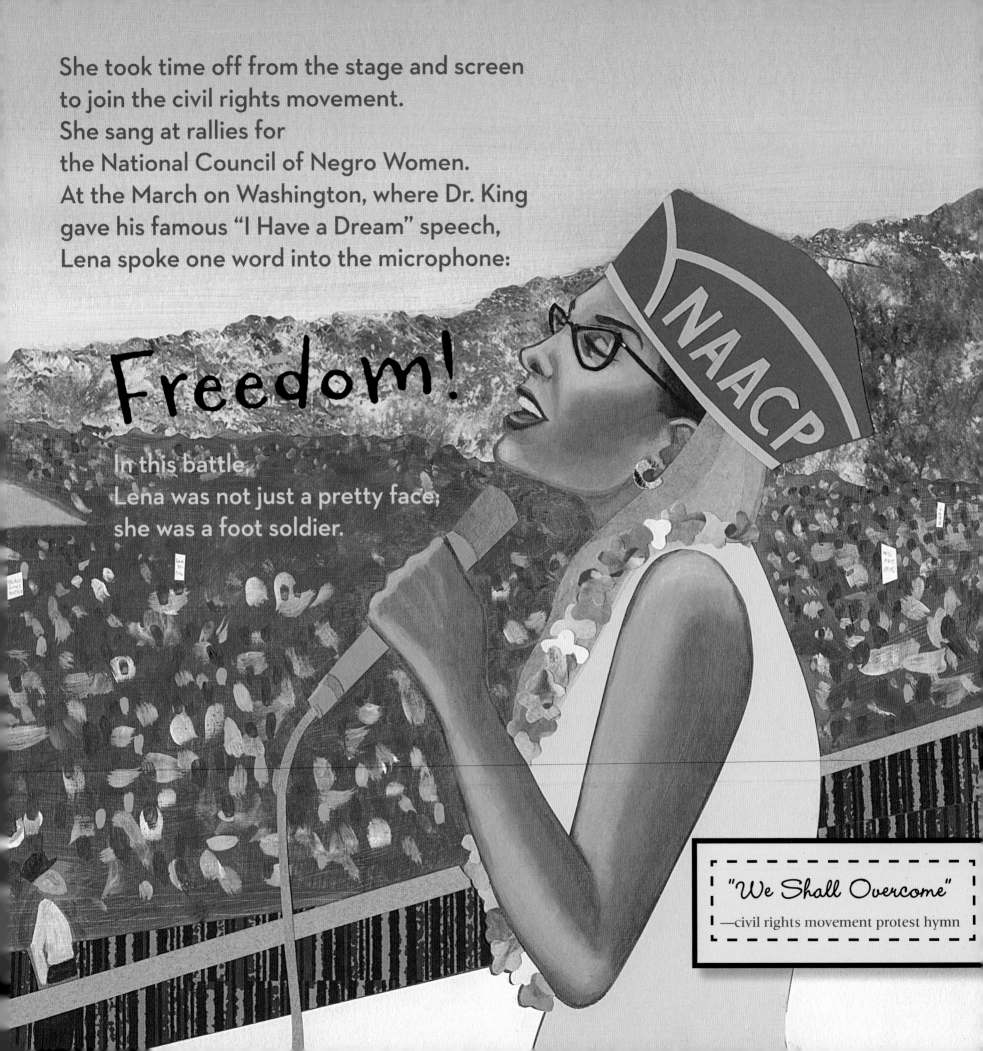

"We Shall Overcome"
—civil rights movement protest hymn

At a 1963 rally with Mississippi civil rights leader Medgar Evers,
Lena sang the spiritual "This Little Light of Mine."
She found not just her voice, but a calling, *her* light.
Days later, Evers was slain. Down but unbowed,
Lena drew on her freedom-fighting roots.

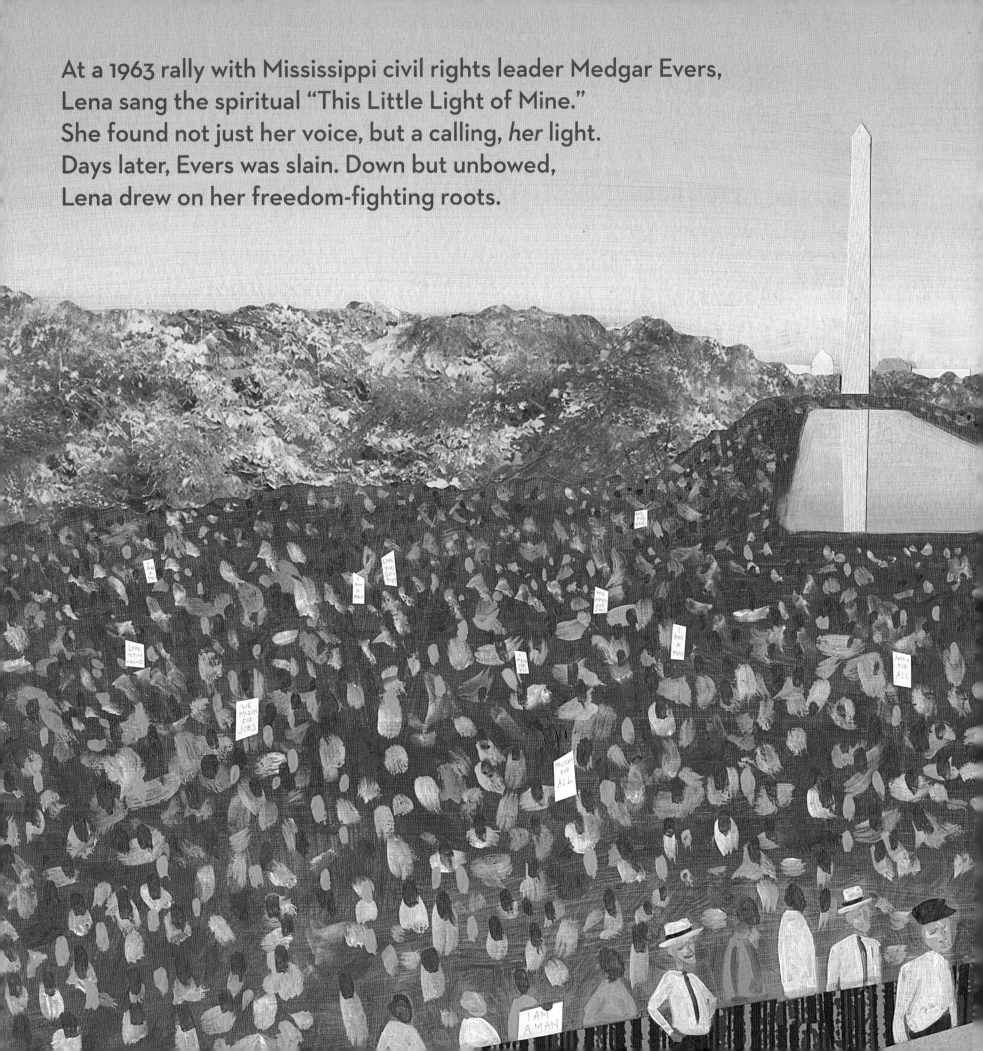

With Lennie at her side, Lena toured nightclubs
and became an international star.
In 1957, her name off the blacklist,
Lena cut records, sang on TV, and starred on Broadway.
But her most important work lay ahead.

Lena kept her tears and her love life to herself.
In 1947 she married Lennie Hayton,
a white music director for MGM.
They married in Paris, France, because many states
in the US did not allow interracial marriage.
Lena and Lennie did not announce their marriage
for three years. She later said that she married
him to advance her career, but she learned to love him.

By then, Lena had married and divorced
and had two children to feed. She had to work.
You got babies, singer Billie Holiday once told her.
You gotta pay your rent.
Like Cora said, *Never let anyone see you cry.*

After World War II, Lena's ties to outspoken activists—
like entertainer Paul Robeson and civil rights leader W. E. B. DuBois—
got her blacklisted. Though not a Communist,
she couldn't get work in Hollywood—
not during Senator Joe McCarthy's Red Scare.
She sang at President Truman's inaugural ball just the same.

So she paid her own way to perform for black troops.
She paid many visits to the base in Alabama
where the famed Tuskegee Airmen
were training to become the first black military aviators.

Although Lena despised Jim Crow laws,
she did her part for the war effort,
singing on armed forces radio shows.
But even the military was segregated.
Just as there were separate bathrooms,
water fountains, and waiting rooms in the South,
there were separate shows—one for black troops
and another for whites.

At one venue, Lena was denied a cup of coffee
but was asked for autographs on her way out.
At another, German prisoners of war
were seated in front of black soldiers.
That indignity was too much for Lena to swallow.
She was fed up with whites-only clubs and theaters.

They didn't make me into a maid,
But they didn't make me into anything else either.

—Lena Horne

Lest Lena be mistaken onscreen for white,
Max Factor created makeup just to darken her skin.
Then she lost roles to white actresses who wore
her makeup to play light-skinned black women.

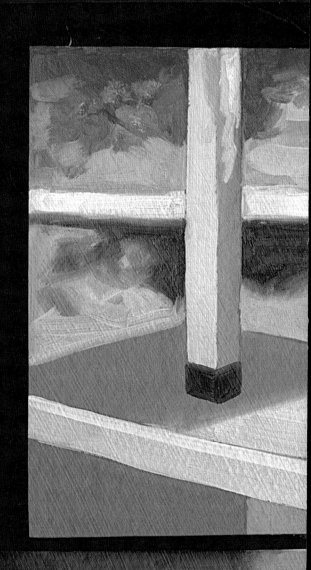

Black moviegoers didn't have it any better than Lena.
Southern theaters that didn't bar blacks
made them use a colored entrance,
sit in the balcony, or wait for midnight screenings.

"Ain't It the Truth?"
—Lena's song from *Cabin in the Sky*

Lena dubbed herself "a butterfly pinned to a column."
She did get to fly in black films like *Cabin in the Sky*
and *Stormy Weather*, whose title song became her anthem.
Even in black-and-white movies, this butterfly dazzled.

Respectable roles, though, were few
for black actresses.
So Lena was cast, instead, in singing numbers
that could be easily snipped from films
when shown in the South
so as not to defy racist views.

But the NAACP wanted Lena
not only to command a paycheck,
but to demand respect.
With the civil rights group behind her,
Lena waged a one-woman war
against stereotypes by refusing to play
maids and mammies onscreen.
NAACP leaders hoped Lena could
change the way that whites saw
African Americans.

When Lena headlined a nightclub out West,
Hollywood studio execs caught her act.
She had already starred in a couple of
low-budget films, including *The Duke Is Tops*.
Now MGM was offering something more—
a studio contract, the first ever
for a black actress.

Touring with the Charlie Barnet Orchestra
was far from glamorous, though.

Lena was banned
from the bandstand between numbers.
Restaurants refused to serve her
and hotels refused her rooms
and she slept in the bus—until Barnet got wise.
He began introducing her as Cuban.
But that didn't take the sting out of racism.

Lena took to the spotlight so well that she was soon fronting an all-white big band—one of the first black vocalists to do so.

Classy as they were, the black band
still had to enter white ballrooms through the back door
and could not stay at white hotels.
For a place to sleep after shows,
band members had to scout for black families
willing to take in a few musicians for a night.

With Sissle, eighteen-year-old Lena cut her first record,
"I Take to You."

NOBLE SISSLE & HIS INTERNATIONAL DANCE ORCHESTRA

WITH LENA HORNE

Before long, Lena leaped from the chorus line
to Broadway in *Dance with Your Gods*.
Then came a singing and dancing gig
with the Noble Sissle Society Orchestra.

Lena auditioned at the fabled Cotton Club.
Harlem's hottest nightspot had valet parking,
sizzling black musical revues, waltzing waiters,
and no mingling between the black performers
and the all-white audience.

I had no talent, said Lena.
All I had was looks.
Just a teen, Lena sashayed
    into the chorus line.
Bandleaders Duke Ellington
and Cab Calloway were now
    her teachers.
Edna chaperoned and
    coached Lena with singing.

Back under Cora's wing in Brooklyn,
Lena attended an integrated all-girls school,
one of the city's best, and joined a debutante social club.

During the Great Depression, Lena left school
and moved in with her mother and new stepfather—
both jobless. As money ran out and bread lines grew,
Lena's mother decided to put her onstage.

"Brother, Can You Spare a Dime?"
—Depression-era song